mama provi
and the
pot of rice

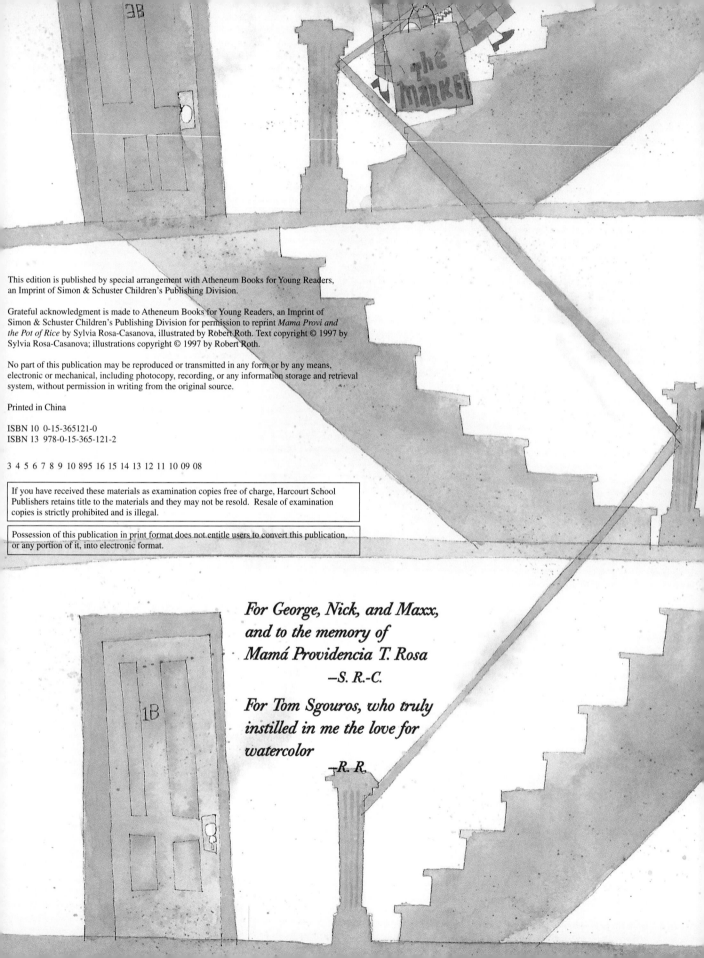

This edition is published by special arrangement with Atheneum Books for Young Readers, an Imprint of Simon & Schuster Children's Publishing Division.

Grateful acknowledgment is made to Atheneum Books for Young Readers, an Imprint of Simon & Schuster Children's Publishing Division for permission to reprint *Mama Provi and the Pot of Rice* by Sylvia Rosa-Casanova, illustrated by Robert Roth. Text copyright © 1997 by Sylvia Rosa-Casanova; illustrations copyright © 1997 by Robert Roth.

Printed in China

ISBN 10 0-15-365121-0
ISBN 13 978-0-15-365-121-2

3 4 5 6 7 8 9 10 895 16 15 14 13 12 11 10 09 08

For George, Nick, and Maxx,
and to the memory of
Mamá Providencia T. Rosa
—S. R.-C.

For Tom Sgouros, who truly
instilled in me the love for
watercolor
—R. R.

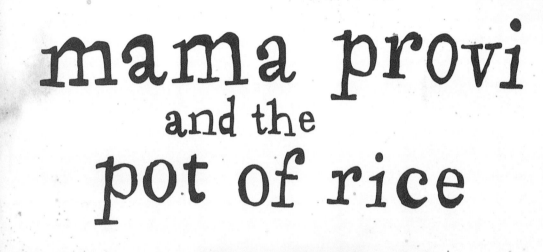

mama provi
and the
pot of rice

by Sylvia Rosa-Casanova

illustrated by Robert Roth

ama Provi lived on the first floor of a tall apartment building. Her granddaughter, Lucy, who was six years old, lived with her parents on the eighth floor of the very same building.

Twice a month, Lucy spent the night at Mama Provi's. They played games and listened to old, scratchy records. At bedtime, Lucy always begged Mama Provi for a story. Mama Provi wove marvelous tales about when she was a little girl growing up in Puerto Rico with her five brothers and four sisters. Lucy fell asleep to stories filled with palm trees, sweet mangoes, and tiny tree frogs called *coquís*.

In the morning, Lucy helped Mama Provi cook breakfast. It was always a tremendous feast because Mama Provi didn't know how to cook for only two people. In her big family, she had been taught to cook for a dozen people at one time.

One Saturday, Lucy's mama called to say that Lucy had the chicken pox and would not be able to visit that evening. Lucy was very sad. Mama Provi wondered what she could do to cheer her up.

Before long, Mama Provi had a wonderful idea. Lucy always said that Mama Provi made the best rice with chicken in the whole world. And so, Mama Provi took out her largest pot and set out to make the most delicious *arroz con pollo* ever.

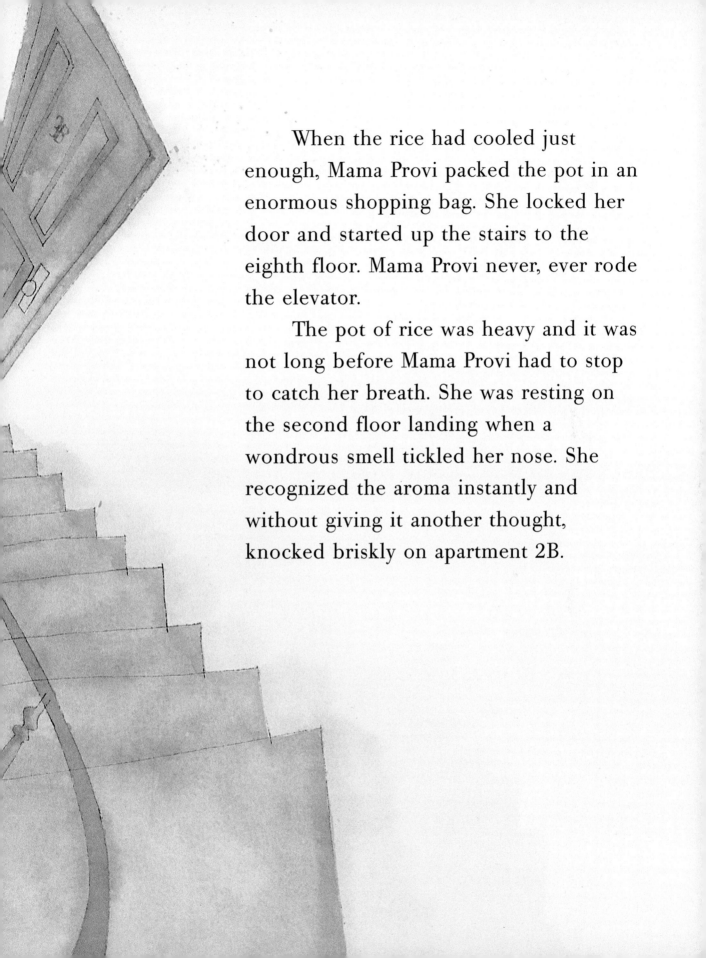

When the rice had cooled just enough, Mama Provi packed the pot in an enormous shopping bag. She locked her door and started up the stairs to the eighth floor. Mama Provi never, ever rode the elevator.

The pot of rice was heavy and it was not long before Mama Provi had to stop to catch her breath. She was resting on the second floor landing when a wondrous smell tickled her nose. She recognized the aroma instantly and without giving it another thought, knocked briskly on apartment 2B.

Mrs. Landers opened the door.

"Excuse me for bothering you, Mrs. Landers, but is that your crusty white bread that I smell?" Mama Provi asked.

Mrs. Landers said it was.

"I wonder if you would trade a bit of your bread for a bowl of my *arroz con pollo*. I am taking this rice to Lucy, who is sick with the chicken pox, and a piece of your bread would go so well with it."

Mrs. Landers was only too pleased to make the trade for she also loved Mama Provi's *arroz con pollo*. *En un dos por tres,* which in Spanish means something like "lickedy-split," Mrs. Landers wrapped up a large chunk of her freshly baked bread and exchanged it for a bowl of Mama Provi's rice.

After thanking Mrs. Landers, Mama Provi continued up the stairs carrying the pot of rice and the chunk of bread.

Mama Provi had not gone very far when she again stopped to catch her breath, this time on the third floor. Again a delightful smell tickled her nose. She recognized the aroma instantly and without giving it another thought, knocked briskly on apartment 3E.

Señor Rivera answered the door.

"Excuse me for bothering you, Señor Rivera, but are those your *frijoles negros* that I smell?" Mama Provi asked.

Señor Rivera said they were.

"I wonder if you would trade a bit of your black beans for a bowl of the *arroz con pollo* I have in this pot. I am taking this rice to Lucy, who is sick with the chicken pox, and your beans would go so well with the rice."

Señor Rivera was only too pleased to make the trade. *En un dos por tres,* he poured a generous helping of his beans into a container and exchanged it for a bowl of Mama Provi's rice.

When Mama Provi reached the fourth floor, she was surprised to find Mrs. Bazzini from apartment 4G waiting for her.

"Mrs. Landers called to tell me that you have a large pot of *arroz con pollo* that you are taking to Lucy," said Mrs. Bazzini. "I was wondering if you would trade a bowl for some of my fresh green salad."

Mama Provi agreed immediately. A nice tossed salad would indeed go very well with her *arroz con pollo*. So, *en un dos por tres*, Mrs. Bazzini exchanged a bowl of salad for a bowl of Mama Provi's rice.

After thanking Mrs. Bazzini, Mama Provi continued up the stairs carrying the pot of rice, the chunk of bread, the container of black beans, and the bowl of salad.

Having given away so much of her rice, Mama Provi was amazed that her shopping bag was still so heavy. She was resting on the fifth floor when a heavenly smell tickled her nose. She recognized the aroma instantly and knocked briskly on apartment 5A.

Mrs. Johnson opened the door.

"Excuse me for bothering you, Mrs. Johnson, but are those your collard greens that I smell?" Mama Provi asked.

Mrs. Johnson said they were.

"I wonder if you would trade a bit of those greens for a bowl of the *arroz con pollo* I have in this pot. I am taking this rice to Lucy, who is sick with the chicken pox, and your collard greens would go so well with the rice."

En un dos por tres, Mrs. Johnson wrapped up a generous portion of her collard greens and exchanged it for a bowl of Mama Provi's rice.

The market

When Mama Provi reached the sixth floor, she bumped straight into Mrs. Woo.

"Mrs. Bazzini called to say that Lucy is ill with the chicken pox," said Mrs. Woo. "Please take this tea to her. I hope it will make her feel better."

Mama Provi asked Mrs. Woo if she would like a bowl of *arroz con pollo* but Mrs. Woo said she would wait until the next time Mama Provi made her tasty rice.

After thanking Mrs. Woo, Mama Provi continued up the stairs carrying the pot of rice, the chunk of bread, the container of black beans, the bowl of salad, the generous portion of collard greens, and the pot of tea.

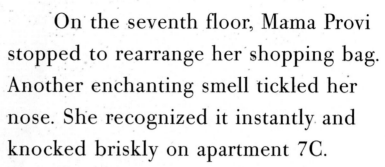

On the seventh floor, Mama Provi stopped to rearrange her shopping bag. Another enchanting smell tickled her nose. She recognized it instantly and knocked briskly on apartment 7C.

Mrs. Kelly answered the door.

"Excuse me for bothering you, Mrs. Kelly, but is that your apple pie that I smell?" Mama Provi asked.

Mrs. Kelly said it was.

"I wonder if you would trade a sliver of your delicious apple pie for a bowl of the *arroz con pollo* I have in this pot. I am taking this rice to Lucy, who is sick with the chicken pox, and your apple pie would make such a nice dessert."

Mrs. Kelly was only too pleased to make the trade and she exchanged a healthy slice of her apple pie for a bowl of Mama Provi's rice.

Although Mama Provi had given away quite a bit of her *arroz con pollo*, her shopping bag was still very heavy. She had finally reached the eighth floor and had stopped to catch her breath when a delicious, heavenly, enchanting, wondrous, delightful odor tickled her nose. It was her *arroz con pollo*, Mrs. Landers's freshly baked bread, Señor Rivera's black beans, Mrs. Bazzini's green salad, Mrs. Johnson's collard greens, Mrs. Woo's tea, and Mrs. Kelly's apple pie. Without giving it another thought, she knocked briskly on apartment 8F.

Lucy answered the door. She was covered with spots.

"Excuse me for bothering you, but are you the little girl who is sick with the chicken pox and cannot come to visit her grandmother?"

Lucy said she was and then hugged Mama Provi as hard as she could.

Mama Provi pointed to the enormous shopping bag. Together they carried it into the apartment and, *en un dos por tres*, they set up a tremendous feast.

"Let's eat!" said Mama Provi.

And that's exactly what they did.